NATIONAL
GEOGRAPHIC

Volcanoes

Monica Halpern

Contents

Introduction

On the Scene at Mount St. Helens

Sunday Evening, May 18, 1980

I woke up to a beautiful Sunday. It was a bright, sunny day. I looked out my window. I could see Mount St. Helens in the distance. The snowcapped mountain shone in the sun. I could see the deep green forests covering its slopes. Below, a crystal clear lake sparkled.

Then, at 8:32 a.m., I heard a tremendous explosion. I was knocked off my feet. I rushed to the window. The volcano had blown! All I could see was a big cloud of gas, ash, and steam. The sky had turned black.

I learned later that the blast was so loud that people 200 miles (322 kilometers) away heard it. The sky was dark for more than 250 miles (402 kilometers).

No one should have been surprised by this blast. Scientists knew it was coming. In March, the mountain began to send out a little steam and ash. Then, a bulge grew on one side of the mountain. The bulge grew bigger and bigger. By mid-May, it looked like a huge blister about to pop.

This isn't the first time that Mount St. Helens has exploded. Native Americans who have lived in the Cascade Mountains for a long time call Mount St. Helens "Fire Mountain." It has blown up five times in the last 280 years. The last time was in 1857.

▲ Scientists kept a watchful eye on the bulge growing on the side of Mount St. Helens.

Monday Evening, May 19, 1980

I continued to watch the mountain send out red-hot rock and steaming mud. I saw rocks thrown high into the air. The hot ash and burning rocks melted the snow. I watched a boiling river of mud race down the mountain. It destroyed everything in its path.

Hot winds blew as hard as winds during a hurricane. They knocked down forests. The flattened trees look like matchsticks. Every living thing in the forest is dead.

The air is still thick with dust and ash. I'm wearing a face mask to protect my lungs.

▼This car was buried under the ash that blew from Mount St. Helens.

Sunday Evening, May 25, 1980

Another smaller blast took place this morning. The sky was dark with ash and smoke again. The street lights came on in some places.

Gray ash covers everything. People are shoveling it out of the streets. Some towns are using snowplows to clear the ash away. The land looks like pictures of the moon. Will anything ever grow here again?

▲The towns near Mount St. Helens were covered in a cloud of ash and smoke after the eruption.

Chapter 1

What Are Volcanoes?

After seeing Mount St. Helens **erupt,** I wanted to learn more about volcanoes. I saw how powerful they were. I saw how much they could destroy. But I wanted to understand what they are and how they form.

A **volcano** is an opening in the Earth out of which melted rock and gases sometimes explode. The word *volcano* refers to the mountain that builds up around this opening. Picture fire gushing out of the top of a mountain. That's what a volcano can look like when it explodes.

Lava gushes from a volcano during a volcanic eruption.

How Volcanoes Form

The Earth is made up of different layers. The thin outer layer is the Earth's **crust**. Below the crust is a hot, thick layer of rock. It's called the **mantle**. Some of the mantle is so hot that its rocks have melted. They have turned into a liquid called **magma**. Below the mantle is the **core**.

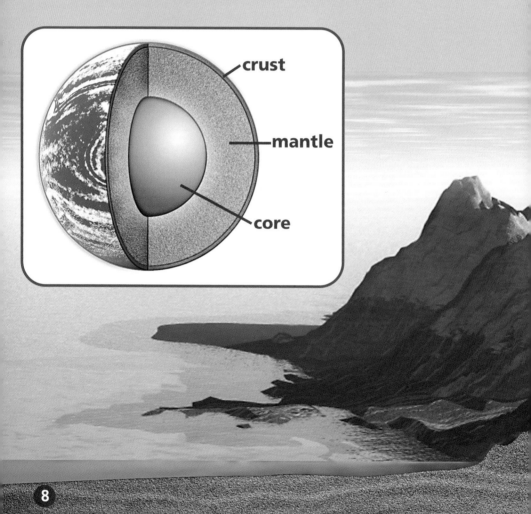

crust

mantle

core

Imagine a steaming, bubbling soup of magma, deep under the surface of Earth. The Earth's crust is not perfectly solid. There are cracks in it. Sometimes, magma bursts through one of these cracks. A volcano is formed. Hot liquid rock, called **lava**, explodes into the air.

Mount St. Helens is a volcano that formed long ago. But once a volcano has formed, another eruption is likely to take place there some day.

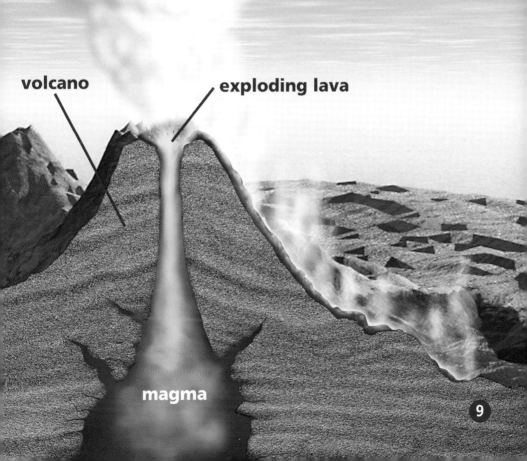

volcano

exploding lava

magma

Types of Volcanoes

I thought that all volcanoes looked alike. But I was wrong. It's true that most volcanoes have the shape of a cone. But volcanoes can actually take three different shapes.

A **shield volcano** is wider than it is high. It is large and rounded. A **composite volcano** looks like a tall mountain. Its peak has steep sides. But its sides are often flatter near its base. It's made up of mixed layers of cinders and lava. A **cinder cone** is a cone-shaped hill. It is much smaller than a shield or a composite volcano. But it has very steep sides.

A shield volcano erupts on one of the Galapagos Islands in Ecuador.

I found out that volcanoes erupt in different ways. Like Mount St. Helens, some explode violently. They blow out hot rocks and ash at over 300 miles (483 kilometers) per hour! These volcanoes usually have steep sides.

Some volcanoes erupt more gently. They produce a runny lava that oozes out and flows down its side. These volcanoes usually spread out over a wide area. They are low and round.

Mount Fuji, in Japan,▶
is a composite volcano.

▼This volcano in Hawaii is a cinder cone.

Chapter 2

Where Are Volcanoes Located?

I was curious to find out where else volcanoes have appeared. I found out that some places on Earth have a lot of volcanoes. Other places have none.

Remember, the outer shell of Earth is called the crust. The crust is broken up into big slabs of rock called **plates**. These plates move around very slowly. Sometimes, the plates push together or pull apart. When that happens, magma can move up between the plates, forming a volcano. Most volcanoes happen at the edges of plates.

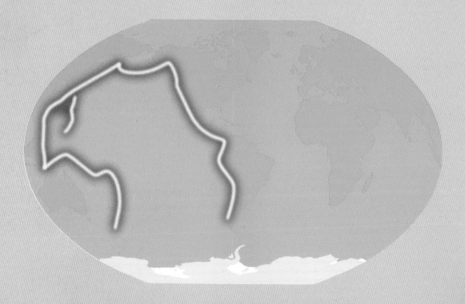

▲ Countries along the edge of the Pacific plate are especially likely to have volcanoes. There are so many volcanoes here that the area is called the "Ring of Fire."

Some volcanoes lie far away from the edges of plates. These places are known as "hot spots." Here, the crust of the Earth is very thin. Magma rises up and bursts through the crust. It forms new volcanoes. Some lie under the ocean. But others have burst out of the ocean to form new islands. The Hawaiian Islands were formed this way.

Some volcanoes are quiet for a long time. But they still show signs of life, such as steam rising. Scientists call these volcanoes **dormant**, which means "sleeping." The volcanoes may erupt again in the future.

If a volcano shows no signs of life for a very long time, it is called **extinct**. Scientists believe that it has stopped erupting. There are about 500 active volcanoes in the world. These volcanoes are not extinct. Only 10 to 20 of them erupt each year.

▼Mauna Loa, in Hawaii, is in a hot spot.

People Who Study Volcanoes

I've learned a lot about volcanoes by talking to scientists who study them. They are called **volcanologists**. These scientists watch how volcanoes act. They also study old rocks and hardened layers of ash from eruptions long ago. From these clues, they can figure out how many times a volcano has erupted.

In 1978, two scientists found that Mount St. Helens was one of the volcanoes in the United States most likely to erupt. They predicted that the volcano might erupt before the year 2000. They were right! Two years later, Mount St. Helens blew up.

Today, scientists are able to predict fairly well when a volcano will erupt. By watching a volcano, they learn to recognize the warnings it gives before erupting. They use several kinds of information to make their predictions. They measure any gases escaping from it. They look for any bulges. They measure the movements of the plates. Small earthquakes near a volcano may mean that an explosion is near.

But no two volcanoes are alike. They act in different ways. A volcano may give many warning signs but never erupt. Other volcanoes erupt without warning.

◀ A volcanologist wears a special suit to study volcanoes up close. The suit protects the volcanologist from the heat.

Chapter 3

Volcanoes in History

Mount St. Helens is a famous volcano of today. But it's interesting to find out about volcanoes of long ago.

Mount Vesuvius

Mount Vesuvius erupted in Italy in the year A.D. 79. It completely buried the nearby city of Pompeii in more than 18 feet (6 meters) of ash. As time passed, Pompeii was forgotten.

The ruins of Pompeii were rediscovered in the 1700s. People worked to uncover the town. They found coins, jewels, and statues. They even found the remains of meals that were left when the volcano erupted.

The rain of hot ash killed many people. Over time, the bodies decayed, leaving hollow shells of hardened ash. Scientists filled these holes with plaster. Then they chipped the hardened ash away. They were able to see what the people looked like.

Today, you can visit the ruins of Pompeii. It is like a city frozen in time. Pompeii shows how powerful and destructive a volcano can be.

Through this arch, you can see Mount Vesuvius. ▶
Today you can still see the position people were in when Vesuvius blew nearly 2,000 years ago.

Krakatau

Mount Vesuvius was only one of the destructive volcanoes of long ago. Another huge disaster was caused by Krakatau. This island volcano in Indonesia blew up in 1883. Some say that the noise of the explosion was the loudest sound in the Earth's history. People as far as 3,000 miles (4,800 kilometers) away heard the explosion.

The explosion blew the island in half. It also caused enormous waves 120 feet (37 meters) high. No one was living on Krakatau. But the waves crashed onto nearby islands where many people lived. More than 36,000 people were swept away.

Waves from Krakatau spread around the world. They hit the coasts of England and France. They hit North and South America. A dust cloud 50 miles (80 kilometers) high traveled around the world.

Famous Volcanoes

Year	Volcano	Place	Estimated Deaths
79	Vesuvius	Italy	16,000
1586	Kelud	Indonesia	10,000
1669	Etna	Italy	20,000
1792	Unzen	Japan	15,000
1815	Tambora	Indonesia	90,000
1883	Krakatau	Indonesia	36,000
1902	Pelée	Martinique	30,000
1985	Nevada del Ruiz	Colombia	23,000

Anak Krakatau is a smaller island volcano that was formed after one of Krakatau's explosions.

Chapter 4

After a Volcano Erupts

After seeing the destruction caused by Mount St. Helens, I knew volcanoes could be harmful. Volcanoes destroy property. Animals and plants die. People can die, too.

Volcanic eruptions can also change the world's weather. A cloud of ash from an eruption can climb more than 7 miles (12 kilometers) high. Some of this ash can stay in the air for more than two years. It can block the sunlight.

Mount Tambora in Indonesia erupted in 1815. In 1816, spring and summer all over the world were cold. People called it the year without a summer. Crops died and many people went hungry.

Volcanoes can be useful, too. Everything may look gray and lifeless after a volcano has blown. But old lava makes very good soil for farming. The lava has many minerals that are good for plants.

The rocks, lava, and other things thrown out by volcanoes have other uses, too. Some are used as building materials. Others are used in cleaning products.

People have found valuable gems and metals around old volcanoes. They have discovered some big diamonds, as well as sapphires and zircons there. Miners have found copper, silver, and gold in old volcanoes, too.

New plants ▶
grow out of
the old lava.

◀ The village of Pinatubo, in the Philippines, was covered in volcanic ash in 1991.

Epilogue

Returning to Mount St. Helens

Well, I had a big question after I saw Mount St. Helens blow up. Would plants and animals ever return to that gray and lifeless place?

I visited the area several years later. I was amazed. Green plants had popped up right in the middle of all the destruction. Flowers were blooming. Insects were buzzing. Birds were singing. Of course, there were no tall trees. It will take many years for the forests to grow back.

Mount St. Helens is still an active volcano. Scientists watch it carefully. They think it will blow up again some day. But that day will probably not come for a long time.

New plants and wildlife began to ▶ appear at Mount St. Helens in the years following the explosion.

Glossary

cinder cone a type of volcano that looks like a cone-shaped hill

composite volcano a type of volcano that is made of layers of cinders and lava and looks like a tall mountain with steep sides

core the thick center of Earth

crust the thin outer layer of Earth

dormant having a time without activity, such as a volcano that is not erupting

erupt to pour or explode out of an opening

extinct no longer alive or active, such as a volcano that scientists think will not erupt in the future

lava hot melted rock on Earth's surface

magma hot melted rock beneath Earth's crust

mantle the thick middle layer of Earth between the crust and the core

plates big slabs of rock that make up Earth's crust

shield volcano a type of volcano with a rounded shape that is wider than it is high

volcano an opening in Earth out of which melted rock and gases sometimes erupt

volcanologists scientists who study volcanoes

Index